T0380856

Carolyn MF Brown

Heart to Heart

credit to: Ramir Quintana

Illustrations by: Ramir Quintana

Introduction

Welcome, to my first book of poems called, "Heart To Heart".

Now, why did I decide to write a book of poems? Well, I wanted
to leave young adults as well as my children and grand-children . . . . .
with a feeling of self -esteem and the capacity to respond within them–selves
emotionally saying . . . yes I can achieve and be the best at
whatever I undertake.

Finally, to give a tribute or dedication to those in my life that have
given me support and guidance. They are my mom, husband, sister,
my pastor and his wife. Gratitude and thank-you all so very much for
your advisement and encouragement to write this book

Now, to you the reader, from my heart to your heart; I sincerely
hope you find my poems enjoyable reading and a time
that was well spent.

Sincerely,
Carolyn MF Brown

Purpose:

Emphasize , the most important gift given to us by "God" is the gift of life. Now, in order to enjoy and appreciate this gift; we as a human race must learn to respect each other through words and deeds regardless at home, work, or at play. If a game is involve; learn the importance of fairness, patience, and understanding. Never be too ashamed to apologize or to say, "I'm sorry". These two words will carry a relationship, even if a family member or a friend a very long way. Remember, that a family is not just a group of people living under one roof;(ex. mom, dad, sibling) but a social unit with a common ancestry which can be traced genealogically. Lastly, learn to love one-self first; then you can reach out to others and love will become much more genuine.

Table of Contents

A Precious Gift

There are so many kinds of gifts today.

Some are big, small for work or play.

Gifts for birthdays and such

Holidays, special days , my.. just so much.

Gifts . . . , coming in many shapes and colors;

Some , arriving in boxes with bows or another

While others are given with a note or a letter

Stating . . .congratulations my friend

Or . . .Gee, I hope you will feel better.

However, the greatest gift I know,

happens not to be tied in a little bow.

But rather wrap with love and care;

That only a dear mother can share.

Now.., I know you are asking; . . . . .

What is this gift, with so much style?

Why, my dear, it's a mother having a "precious child".

Any Child with Love

Who has eyes as bright as stars above

Lay slumbering peacefully as a dove;

Then suddenly awakens and smothers you with love?

Only my friend, any child with love.

Who is always ready with open arms

To say " I love you" with such charm;

Then give hugs and kisses and mean no harm?

Only my friend, any child with love.

Well, as you can see, in reaching a conclusion;

There is simply no room for any delusion.

For there is nothing on earth or heaven above,

As precious as . . ."any child with love".

Born with a good Heart

Mothers!, children will be children no matter what you say or do

For they are "God's" little creatures and

Only "He" can make their dreams come true.

But first, children must become adults and stand the test of time.

Of course, some will become industrious;

While others, sadly, will prefer doing crimes.

Some will become lawyers and preachers;

Others, doctors and teachers too.

While others will become laborers and parents just like you.

However, no matter what goal your child may choose

Or how his or her life may start;

Remember, he or she was once your little child

Now , ...adult, "Born with a good Heart".

A Child's Prayer

My father, as I begin to lay down to sleep;

I pray to you, my soul you will keep.

For if I should die, before I awake

Please, I pray my soul you will take.

God, please bless my mother and my dad;

My brother and sister too . . . just

Because they all love you as much as I really do.

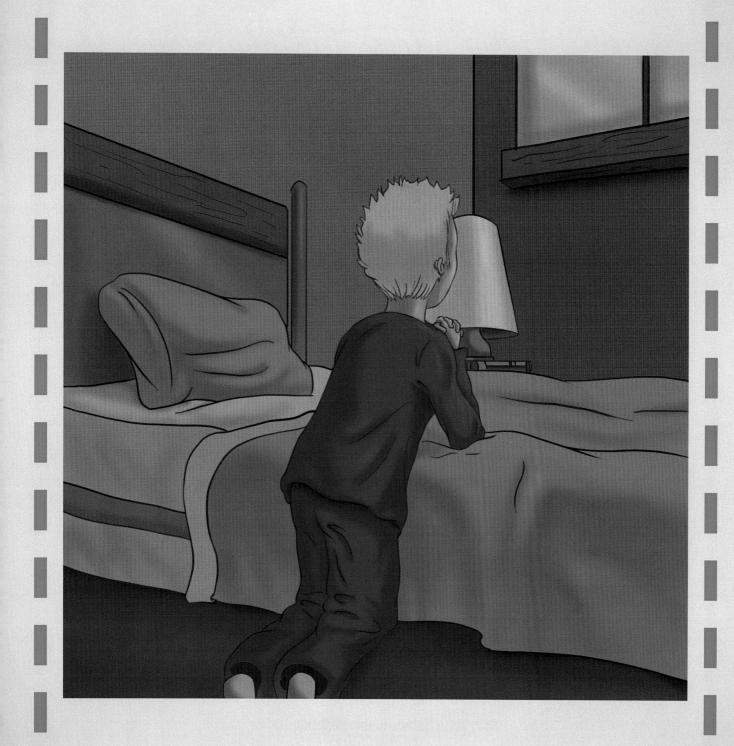

A Child's Lullaby

Chorus:

Hush, little baby......hush, hush....
Hush, little ba-by....hush, hush....

Song:

Now the day is over, night is drawing nigh.
Clouds of the evening, steal across the sky
When the sky and clouds darken;
stars will begin to peep.....
You, my child and nature will soon be asleep.

But when the morning awakens;
then you, my child and nature will rise.
Pure, beautiful and lovely;
In God's holy eyes......

Chorus:

Hush, little baby...Hush, Hush
Hush, little baby...Hush, Hush...sh....hush

14

How to Respect a Friend

Respond apologetically when necessary;

Even though that friend may not like your advice.

Still, if you can, give a friendly hug for therapy.

Plan events, movies or plays together is a high measure.

By all means . . .

Engage in a friendly conversation that's pleasurable

For being earnest is a state of mind

So

Connect by staying in touch, shows you are very kind.
..
Why? simply because . . . .

Tenderness or compassion is what a friend expects;

Especially when one is showing

Respect.!!!!

Mother

This bouquet of flowers that you see;

I give especially to you from me.

To express my appreciation for you and to tell you that I admire you too.

From your modesty of behavior and style;

To your virtuous nature and pleasant smile.

I could always count on you to be by my side; as well as be my steadfast guide.

So again, "mother", to honor you on this day;

I bestow you with this special bouquet.

Symbolizing how much I care

and expressing my thank-you,

For all the happy moments we shared.

This poem was written
For my mom in May, "07; she died in August, "08.

My Husband

Reginald,

my Love,

&

Close Friend;

I Give

Love

&

Kisses!!!!

Why?

Let's just say my hubby, you will always be my heart.
Well,.. hey, I knew you would be from the start.
Because of your caring and understanding; to you I say,
Gee, you brighten up each and everyday.

My Sister

Has always been there for me;

Through my good days, bad days, or

Just my simple need for a new recipe.

She is the type of person , that takes life with stride, why?

Simply, because she has much pride.

However , regardless of wherever I go

Or whatever I do

She will always be apart

Of me . . . . .

And very, very close to my heart.

This poem is very special to me because on Sept,'01 my sister gave me her kidney. Thank-you, sis.

A Father & A Pastor

There are similarities between these two;

For they both teach, give guidance , express concern and compassion as well as show much humility too.

Neither was born by birthright or by blood;

Yet they both have one thing in common . . . .

A heart full of love

One is direct and strong in discipline, especially

If his child should stumble or fall.

While the other, preaches to his church family;

That "God" is the answer and hears when we call.

Now who is this person that possess these beautiful qualities which seem to come together as a clone?

Why, my friend and pastor, Rev. Arthur M. Jones.

A Pastor's Wife

A promise of love from my heart do I give.

Always steadfast as long as I live.

Secure of the mind will I be;

Though hills and valleys of life do I see.

Obstacles may come, but I remain by your side;

Ready and willing always to be your guide.

Courageous and virtuous woman, I am in this life;

Why?, because I am a "Pastor's wife.

Happy Easter / It's Springtime

Easter is also a holiday that arrives in spring.

When "Mother Nature" begins to revive everything.

Why, you can see new arrivals everywhere;

From the budding of flowers and trees,

To colorful butterflies flying here and there.

Easter, my friend is also a time to start;

Reflecting on desires and passions of the heart.

Caring no longer about the past;

But concentrating only on relationships that may last.

Having someone, or that special someone by your side;

That will lend a helping hand or simply be your guide..

So, may I, in forming a conclusion just say:

In order to have a productive day;

Go out and breathe a breath of fresh air.

Shucks, let the wind mess-up that perfect hair.

After all, being out of place is not a crime,

You are just having a "Happy Easter/,It's Springtime!!

A Mother's Day Wish

Mom, of all the gifts you have given me;
Of all of which I am bless.
Your gift of my roots, I cherish foremost the very best.

Because you set my roots in such endearing love and then nourished them with tender care;
Knowing in your heart, the fruits, good or bad my roots could sometimes bear.

I hereby grant this "Mother's Day Wish", . . . yes especially for you;
May you have a joyful and delightful day;
regardless of what you pursue.

For I can see plainly now, that life has not turned you cold;
But only made your love grow stronger, in a heart;
Oh my, ... made of precious gold.
Happy "Mother's Day!"

This Father's Day

(A Proud Father)

Well, the road has not been easy;

as you my son and daughter

can plainly see.

Economic conditions has almost

taken the very best of me.

Rising cost here

and raising of taxes there;

Almost make any man shrug his shoulders

and proclaim loudly;

I...just......don't......care.!!!!!

But at the end of each and everyday,

when I began to settle down;

reflecting on day to day problems all around,

I begin to realize on this day, Father's Day;

my life, truly isn't after all a bother.

For I do have a wonderful family and I am

very, very, happy to say, "a proud father."

Happy Father's Day to all father's and father's to be.!!

Copyright © 2011 by Carolyn MF Brown. 93055-BROW

ISBN: Softcover 978-1-4653-9030-1

All rights reserved. No part of this book may
be reproduced or transmitted in any form or by
any means, electronic or mechanical, including
photocopying, recording, or by any information
storage and retrieval system, without permission
in writing from the copyright owner.

To order additional copies of this book, contact:
Xlibris Corporation
1-888-795-4274
www.Xlibris.com
Orders@Xlibris.com

Printed in the United States
By Bookmasters